KEEPING PETS

Horses and Ponies

Tristan Boyer Binns

Heinemann
LIBRARY

www.heinemann.co.uk/library
Visit our website to find out more information about Heinemann Library books.

To order:
☎ Phone 44 (0) 1865 888066
▤ Send a fax to 44 (0) 1865 314091
▯ Visit the Heinemann bookshop at www.heinemann.co.uk/library to browse our catalogue and order online.

First published in Great Britain by Heinemann Library, Halley Court, Jordan Hill, Oxford OX2 8EJ, part of Harcourt Education.

Heinemann is a registered trademark of Harcourt Education Ltd.

Editorial: Andrew Farrow and Stig Vatland
Design: Richard Parker and Q2A Solutions
Illustrations: Jeff Edwards
Picture Research: Maria Joannou and Virginia Stroud-Lewis
Production: Chloe Bloom

Originated by Modern Age Repro
Printed and Bound in China
by South China Printing Company

10 digit ISBN: 0 431 12429 9 (Hardback)
13 digit ISBN: 978 0 431 12429 2

10 digit ISBN: 0 431 12456 6 (Paperback)
13 digit ISBN: 978 0 431 12456 8

10 09 08 07 06
10 9 8 7 6 5 4 3 2 1

British Library Cataloguing in Publication Data
Binns, Tristan Boyer
Horses and ponies. - (Keeping pets)
1.Horses - Juvenile literature
636.1

A full catalogue record for this book is available from the British Library.

Acknowledgements
The publishers would like to thank the following for permission to reproduce photographs: Alamy Images pp. **9 bottom** (Cosmo Condina), **19 bottom right** (geogphotos), **19 top** (Holt Studios International Ltd), **10** (Peter Titmuss), **19 bottom left** (Photofusion Picture Library), **14** (Russ Merne), **9 top** (Terry Fincher Photo Int); Bob Langrish p. **21**; Getty Images (Stone) pp. **5 top**, **6**; Harcourt Education Ltd (Tudor Photography) pp. **4**, **8**, **11 bottom**, **11 top**, **12**, **16**, **17**, **20 bottom**, **20 top**, **22 bottom**, **22 top**, **23 bottom**, **23 top**, **24 bottom**, **24 left**, **24 right**, **25**, **26**, **27**, **28 bottom**, **28 top**, **29**, **30**, **31 bottom**, **31 top left**, **31 top right**, **32**, **33**, **34 top**, **35 bottom**, **36 bottom**, **36 top**, **37 bottom**, **37 top**, **38**, **39 right**, **41 bottom**, **41 top**, **43 bottom**, **44**, **45**; Kit Houghton Photography pp. **15**, **35 top**, **39 left**, **42**, **43 top**; NHPA pp. **7 bottom** (Henry Ausloos), **7 top** (Joe Blossom); Science Photo Library (David Aubrey) p. **5 bottom**.

Cover photograph reproduced with permission

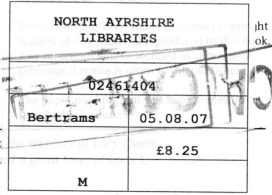

This book is dedicated to ... *a friend, a colleague a* ...

Contents

Any words appearing in the text in bold, **like this**, are explained in the Glossary.

What is a horse or pony?

Horses and ponies today come from wild **herd** animals first tamed about 6,000 years ago. In the wild they lived in all sorts of places, from seashores to mountains to grassy plains. Today you will still find horses and ponies in many different places.

Horses and ponies are **herbivores**, so they eat grass and other plants. They are **mammals**. This means they are **warm-blooded**, give birth to live babies, and feed the babies milk. They are part of a group of animals with hooves that includes donkeys and zebras.

What is the difference?

Horses and ponies are measured to their withers, a spot where the neck joins the back. They are often measured in **hands**. A hand is 10 cm (4 in). Sometimes they are measured in metres. A pony measures up to 14.2 hands (1.47 m, 52 in).

A horse and a pony may be very different sizes, but they came from the same **ancestors** long ago.

Still wild

- There are still wild horses and ponies all over the world.
- American Mustangs and Australian Brumbies are now wild, but they came from tamed horses that escaped between 200 and 500 years ago.
- The oldest type of wild pony in England is the Exmoor pony.

Wild Mustangs are sometimes rounded up and given to good homes.

Exmoor ponies are one of the many types of wild pony in the world.

Need to know

- In every country, there are laws about owning animals.
- You must care for your animals the right way. You are responsible for keeping them healthy and happy.
- If you do not look after them properly, you are breaking the law and can be arrested.
- Large animals such as horses and ponies can only be kept where there is enough space.
- Your local council will have rules on how much land is required to keep one.

Horse and pony facts

The best way to understand horses and ponies is to see how they live in the wild. They live in a **herd.** They spend most of their time walking and **grazing**. Each day, the average horse eats about 10 kilograms (22 pounds) of grass and drinks about 30 litres (8 gallons) of water, but spread out over the whole day. They have small stomachs, which are ideal for this slow but steady eating. You will need to keep this in mind when you feed your horse. Their very long **intestines** let them get all the **nutrients** out of the grass before passing the waste out as droppings.

Each herd usually has only one stallion. He drives others away.

Happy in herds

Every herd has a **pecking order.** This means that each animal has its place, with the leader being the most important. When a new horse comes into the herd, it has to find its place in the pecking order. They sometimes fight to work this out.

Horses and ponies are happiest in groups. They will **groom** each other with their lips and teeth. They use their tails to swish flies away from each other. One will look out for danger while others rest. A horse or pony kept on its own soon gets unhappy. You will need to have an animal friend for your own horse.

Every pony in this herd knows where he or she belongs.

Horses look after each other in the wild and when they are kept by people.

Did you know?

- Horses can live to between 20 and 35 years.
- Adult males are called stallions, or **geldings** if they have been **neutered.**
- Adult females are called mares.
- Horses have one baby at a time. Babies are called **foals.**
- Female foals are called fillies and male foals are called colts.
- An adult Falabella (miniature horse) can weigh as little as 18 kilograms (40 pounds), while a large horse such as a Shire can weigh over a tonne!

7

Teeth and hooves

Horses are **grazing** animals and their teeth are perfect for eating grass. They should wear down evenly and slowly through the animal's lifetime. You can tell roughly how old a horse or pony is by looking at the patterns of wear in its teeth.

The hooves wear slowly as the animal walks. Most horses and ponies walk and trot in the wild but only gallop when in danger. This means their legs, feet, and hooves are best suited for going slowly. If you ride on roads, jump, or go at speed for any length of time, your horse will need shoes.

Danger!

If there is danger in the wild, horses run away from it. They can go from standing still to running at full speed very quickly. If one horse is startled or alarmed, he will alert the **herd** and they will all run together. Even newborn **foals** can run quickly very soon after they are born. If they are cornered, horses and ponies can fight with their hooves and teeth. They can rear up and plunge down on an attacker, or kick out quickly with great force. Be careful not to startle a horse or you could get this kind of reaction, too.

As soon as a foal is born, both it and its mother are ready to run if they need to.

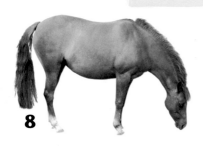

Babies

Mares are pregnant for eleven months. They have one foal at a time. When a foal is born, it can stand and run almost immediately. In the wild they need to be able to run from danger as soon as they are born. After about six months, they do not need their mother's milk any more. They are not adults though until they are between three and six years old, depending on their breed.

Horse senses

Horses and ponies have very good senses of hearing and smell. They can hear sounds of danger or smell friends. They can see almost all the way around their bodies, except for a blind spot at the very back. They use their sense of taste to make sure their food is safe to eat.

These are heavy horses. Horses like these have been used to pull ploughs and work on farms for thousands of years.

Racing is done in many ways in different parts of the world, but it is always exciting.

Outside and in

Because they live outdoors all the time in the wild, most horses and ponies are happiest outdoors. They can survive in a wide range of weather conditions. In really wet and windy conditions, or if it is hot and humid, they need shelter. Make sure your horse has a shelter in its field or **paddock**. If you keep your horse in a stable some of the time, make sure it gets to spend some of every day outside in a field. Being kept indoors all the time can make a horse feel bored and unhappy. Then it may behave badly or get sick.

Horses and ponies can sleep standing up. They lock their legs to hold them up. This standing sleep is a light sleep. They need to lie down to sleep deeply, but they only do this for about half an hour at a time. In order to lie down, the animal needs to feel safe. A horse or pony can relax if it is watched over by its **herd** in the field or if it is in a familiar **loose-box.**

Even small ponies can pull carts. Ponies used to pull coal in mines.

So much choice

Horses and ponies come in a wide range of sizes, colours, and types. People use them for many things, from driving and farming, to riding and racing. Horses, ponies, and people can work together very well to have fun and make each other's lives better.

Welsh Mountain ponies are up to 12 **hands** high and come in any solid colour. They are great ponies for children.

Horse sounds

Horses and ponies use a wide range of sounds. They can neigh to warn others and whinny or whicker to show they like you. They may snort (make a blowing sound) to show they are excited or having fun.

Grey horses such as this thoroughbred can be hard to keep clean! Greys have black skin. Many horses that look black are actually dark brown or grey.

11

Is a horse or pony for you?

Most horse and pony owners cannot imagine life without their animals. They are great fun to get to know, and looking after them means you get fresh air and exercise as well! But horses also need constant care. Think carefully about these things before you decide to get a horse or pony of your own. Your family will need to be supportive, since you will need their help and money. It may even be possible to have riding lessons at a local stable without having your own horse.

You never stop learning about and training your horse or pony. This keeps it exciting.

Add it up

Horses and ponies will always cost a lot of money to keep. It can cost more to keep one for a year than it costs to buy it. Think about expenses such as food, housing, **tack**, and equipment. You will often need to use experts such as the vet for routine checkups and **vaccinations** and the **farrier** for shoes and hoof trimming. You should also save money for emergencies.

Horse and pony good points

- They live for 20 to 35 years, so your friend should be around for a long time.
- You will get to know each other very well. An animal can be a special friend that is always happy to see you.
- Riding grows more interesting when you and your horse work together over a long period of time.
- Exercise and fresh air keep you healthy, too!

Horse and pony not-so-good points

- The average horse eats 10 kilograms (22 pounds) of grass or hay and drinks 30 litres (8 gallons) of water a day. You will need to make sure yours gets the right amount every day.
- They need exercise and **grooming** every day.
- The vet will need to visit once or twice a year.
- The farrier should come every six to eight weeks.
- The field and stall they live in will need to be cleaned every day.
- Some people are very **allergic** to horses and ponies.
- They need a lot of space. A field with a shelter, or a **paddock** and stabling, are necessary. If you do not have space at home, you will need to keep your horse at a **livery stable,** which can be expensive, too.
- It takes a lot of work and equipment to keep horses and ponies happy and healthy.

Choosing your pony

So, you and your family have decided to get a horse or pony. Congratulations! Now you have to make some decisions. It is a good idea to learn to ride before you get your own horse or pony. What kind of riding do you want to do? Do you want to go for rides in the countryside, or do you want to compete at something like show jumping or eventing? Talk to your riding instructor about what breed and size of pony is right for you.

Are you going to want to take your horse or pony to shows? You may want to buy a **registered pedigree** so you can take it to special shows for its breed. Or you may want to choose a mixed breed. They are usually less expensive. They can have the best qualities of both breeds. You can think about getting a rescued horse or pony from a **shelter.** Many rescued ponies have been mistreated and may not be easy to care for. You may want to wait until you have more experience before taking on a rescued horse. Ask your local shelter for advice.

A great way to show off speed and skill is Western-style barrel racing. Quarter horses are good barrel racing and general Western **reining** horses.

Timing

If you think that you will not have enough time to care for your horse or pony by yourself, you could find someone to share it with. Another idea is to keep it at a riding school for free in return for letting it be used in riding lessons.

Begin your search

When you have decided these things, you can start looking for your horse or pony. Adverts in local papers, the Internet, local breeders, and your riding school are all good places to start looking. Find an expert to help you when you go to see a possible choice. If your riding instructor could help, that would be ideal. He or she already knows how you ride and what is best for you.

Not yet ready?

You may not be ready to have your own horse or pony yet. You can still learn a lot from books and magazines. Taking riding lessons and helping out at local stables are great ways to get experience. You can join clubs, such as the Pony Club. You do not have to own a horse or pony to join in. Look on page 47 for contact information.

Pony Club shows are perfect for children. As you improve, you can enter more difficult classes.

Check it out

When you go to see a horse or pony you are thinking of buying, it is best to take an expert to help you check everything. Check its body to make sure it is healthy. The legs and feet are very delicate. You need to make sure there are no problems that could cause **lameness.** Before you agree to buy the horse, you should ask your vet to examine it, too.

A well-built horse is said to have good **conformation.** The horse or pony should be **trotted out** by someone running alongside holding the lead rope. Its legs should swing freely and it should not **favour** any of its feet. It should be eager, but not too excitable.

You should watch someone else ride it and see how it walks, trots, canters, and gallops. Then you should ride it yourself. Are you comfortable? Does it listen to your commands? How well trained is it? Do you have the time and skill to keep training it?

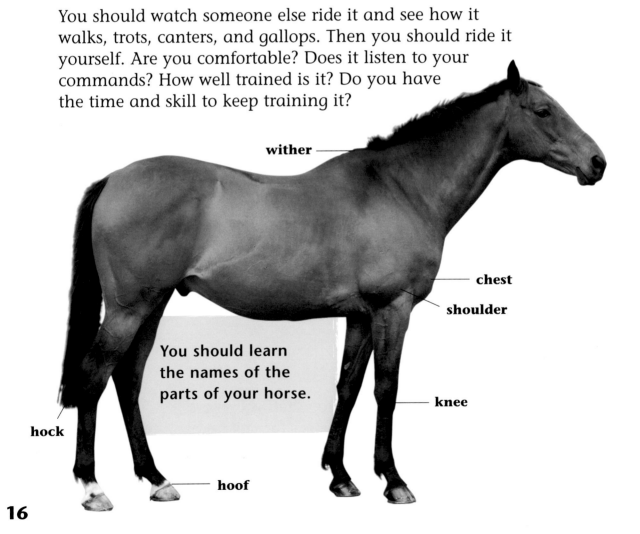

wither

chest

shoulder

You should learn the names of the parts of your horse.

knee

hock

hoof

frog

A healthy hoof. The **frog** absorbs impact as the foot touches the ground, like a shock absorber.

sole

Happy or not?

Finally watch as the horse or pony is let loose, or "turned out", in its field. Is it calm but interested in the world around it? A horse or pony should have its ears pricked forward most of the time. This shows it is alert and thinking. Ears laid back against the head mean it is angry or scared and may bite or kick. A happy horse or pony walks or trots into a field, obviously pleased to be there and to see its friends again. It may roll on the ground. Unhealthy animals go slowly and gingerly. They do not pay attention to the world around them. Their heads may hang, and they may clamp their tails close into their bodies.

Top tip

Watch out for a horse or pony that is very hard to catch in the field. This behaviour can cost you time. It could also be dangerous in an emergency.

Bad habits

Some horses and ponies have bad habits. A horse or pony may walk away as you try to mount it or rub its head hard along your body as you stand next to it. As you ride, it may keep dropping its head to grab bites of grass. In the stable, it may bite its door and suck air up. This is called "cribbing". These habits can be hard to break.

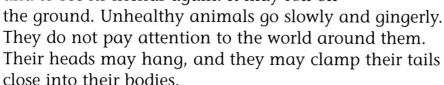

What do I need?

Most horses are happy living outside all the time. But usually people keep their horses outdoors for part of the time and stabled for the rest. What you choose will depend on where you live, how much money you have, and what you like. Your horse or pony may be kept at your home or in a **livery stable.** If you do not own any land, you can rent it. If you move your horse around, to go to a show for example, you will also need to use a horsebox or trailer. Talk about this with your family. You can find more information from experts, books, and Internet sites.

Poisonous plants

- Generally, horses do not eat plants that can make them sick. But a hungry or bored animal may try to eat anything.
- Find out from your local council, vet or riding stables what poisonous plants are common where you live.
- Get a list with pictures and go out into your pasture.
- When you find a poisonous plant, make sure you dig it out, including the roots.
- Keep a watchful eye on where it grew to make sure it doesn't come back. Some plants take years to get rid of!

Staying outside

Ideally, you should have about 1 hectare (2.5 acres) of **pasture** for each animal. If it can be close to a house where people live it will be safer, since thieves will be afraid of being seen. Split the pasture in half with a fence, so one part can be **grazed** while the other is rested. After a while, move the horses into the rested half. This lets the grass recover. It also means the horses get fewer **parasites.** Because horses and ponies are **herd** animals, they should have other animals in the field with them.

Checking the field

Before you put any animals in a field, you need to check it over to make sure it is safe. Look for poisonous plants, broken glass, plastic bags, cans, droppings from other animals, and other junk. You should clear the field regularly to make sure nothing has grown back or been dumped in it. Regularly clear up the droppings from your animals so the field does not get infested with parasites.

ragwort

Here are some plants that are poisonous to horses and ponies.

bracken

oak leaf and acorn

Field rules

Fencing is important. It keeps your animals in their field, so it keeps them safe. Good fencing must not hurt your horses, so barbed wire is never a good choice. Simple board fencing is best. Electrified wire can work well, too. Wood fencing makes it harder for a thief to steal your horse. Whatever you use, make sure it is checked regularly, and repaired as soon as it is damaged. Gates should swing easily and have pony-proof locks.

There should be a field shelter to protect your horses from extreme wind, rain, snow, sun, and heat. A good field shelter should have three sides, or four with a wide doorway. It needs to be solid and leakproof, since it is meant to protect your horse in bad weather. You should clear droppings out of the field shelter every day or so.

Any horse would enjoy this fine **pasture** and field shelter.

Big stables usually open into a covered central passageway or onto a fenced and gated yard.

Living in

Stables come in many different styles and sizes. Good stables should all have the following things, no matter how different they look.

- A **loose-box** should be big enough for your pony to turn around and lie down in. It should have splinter-free walls and good airflow without draughts. The door should be divided into two sections, so the horse can look out over the top. Each stable needs a hay net or manger. You will need a bucket or trough if you feed your horse **grain** as well.

- An easy to clean, non-slip floor made from something that will not rot such as roughened concrete.

- There should be somewhere under cover for you to **groom** your horse and a secure ring to tie lead ropes to.

- There should be a secure, dry storage area for feed and bedding.

- You need running water – for your horse, to wash your hands, and to wash your equipment.

- Lighting is important – security lights that go on when they sense movement help keep the place safe. There should also be bright, covered lights all around the stables so you can work after dark.

- You need a place to keep your **tack** and other equipment tidy and safe, and to clean it after use.

Top tip

People usually have **insurance** to cover emergency bills. Insurance usually pays out if a horse is hurt or unexpectedly ill. Treatments for horses can be very expensive, so you should always have insurance.

This is an ideal loose-box, all ready for its pony to come home. However, even the nicest stable or stall is not suitable for a horse to be kept in all day and night.

Bedding

Whenever you keep a horse or pony in a stable, you need to put down bedding to keep it safe and comfortable. Many people use wood shavings or straw. Depending on where you are, you may be able to try other things such as **hemp** or shredded paper. Remember that bedding takes up a lot of space. You need to think about how it will be delivered and stored.

Storing food

Some people will have enough **pasture** to feed their horses without having to give them any **grain** as well. But almost everyone will need to feed their horse hay at some point. When the grass is not growing in the winter, horses can run out of **grazing** in a pasture. So you will need a dry, well-ventilated space to store hay bales. You usually get many months' worth of hay in one delivery, so this storage space may need to be very big!

Wood shavings.

Shredded paper.

Grain needs to be kept in containers that animals cannot get into. You can use rubbish bins with tight-fitting lids. They need to be kept somewhere dry and cool.

Top tip

Horses and ponies love grain and can be very clever about finding it. They do not know when to stop eating. If a horse or pony eats too much grain, or even too much new spring grass, it cannot vomit it out. Instead, it gets colic. Colic is like an upset stomach, but it can kill a horse or pony.

A drinking trough in a field can be far away from the nearest tap, so plan how you will get water to it carefully.

Water

Horses and ponies drink lots of water every day, so they must always be able to get to some. Each field and stable needs a supply of clean, fresh water. An easy way to do this is to use automatic waterers. These are like water fountains that refill themselves as they get drained. Buckets and hosepipes work just as well, but they mean more work for you. However you water your animals, make sure the troughs and buckets are scrubbed out regularly to keep them clean.

23

Basic needs

Now you can think about all the other things that you need to care for your pony. To keep the stable and field clean you will need a wheelbarrow, forks, and rakes for **mucking out.** To keep the horse clean, you will need brushes and combs, a hoof pick, and sponges. In the **pasture**, your horse may need a rug to keep warm. A headcollar and lead rope let you catch and lead your pony safely. To ride, you need a saddle and bridle as well as saddle soap and sponges to keep your **tack** clean. You will also need stable clothes, riding clothes, and waterproof boots. Finally, you should have horse and human first aid kits in case of an emergency.

If you start going to shows, the list of equipment you need can grow very long! You may be able to share, borrow, or rent some of it. This is true of some other stable equipment, too. If you do borrow anything, make sure you understand how to use it and give it back clean.

Believe it or not, you may need all this equipment to look after just one horse or pony!

A small stable set up such as this one is an ideal place to keep a few ponies.

24

Exercise

It is best to vary exercise a bit to keep you and your pony interested. An indoor riding arena is wonderful for lessons and serious work, whatever the weather. An outdoor ring, with a solid fence and well-drained level surface, works very well, too. Most riders and ponies love riding in the countryside on **bridlepaths.**

Horses need exercise every day.

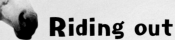

Riding out

- Always tell someone where you are going and when you expect to be back.
- Stick to the path and do not cut across private land.
- Shut any gates securely behind you.
- Do not alarm other animals, for instance by galloping through fields of cows or sheep.
- If you can, carry a mobile phone with you.
- Never ride out alone. Even the most experienced riders and unshakeable ponies have accidents.

Caring for your horse

Some animals need more food than others to stay at the right weight. Ask your vet if your pony is too thin, too heavy, or just right. Then change his diet to work towards getting him to a healthy weight. Your horse may also need more or less food at different times of the year or if the amount of work he does varies.

You may use a combination of these feeds for your horse or pony.

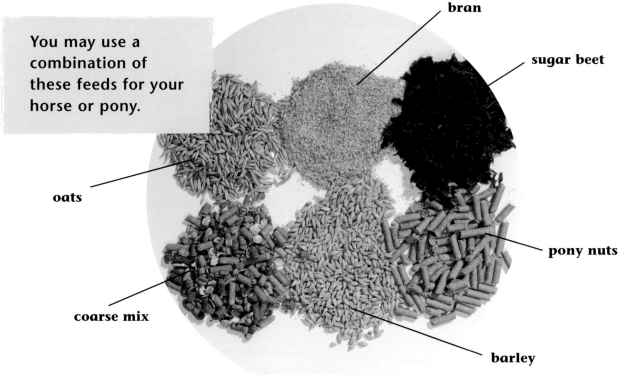

bran

sugar beet

oats

pony nuts

coarse mix

barley

What to feed

The bulk of any horse's diet should be grass and hay. If he is doing a lot of work, or needs to eat a great deal to keep his weight up, you may need to add **hard feeds** as well. Hard feeds are **grains**, such as oats, barley, and maize. You can use single grains or buy ready-mixed feeds. These are called pony nuts, pony cubes, and coarse mix. They are a good choice for most animals and owners because they already have the right balance of **nutrients.** If you change types of feed, do it slowly. A sudden change can upset your horse's stomach.

You should always feed the same amounts of food at the same times each day. Weigh or measure the hard feed and hay you give each time to make sure it is the right amount. Horses and ponies love routine. They get **stressed** if their schedules change, even if it is the weekend! It is best to give horses hard feed twice a day, but never before or right after exercise. They should always have water and hay or grass available. A haynet helps to keep hay off the ground, so it does not get trampled and wasted.

Good hay looks green to light brown, smells fresh and sweet, and has no mould or wet patches. Check each bale before you feed it to your horse, since bad hay can make it very sick.

Treats

Treats are great ways to reward good behaviour or say thanks for a fun ride. Do not give too many treats, or at the same times every day as your pony may start to expect them and nip you. Good treats, such as carrots, turnips, and apples can even help keep a horse healthy. Watch out though – too many apples can give it colic.

Sweets

Never give a horse sweets or fizzy drinks. Horses are not meant to eat sugar and it can rot their teeth and upset their stomachs.

Fresh water

A horse should always have access to fresh water in her stable or field. If you do not have an automatic waterer, top up the field troughs once a day. Scrub them out whenever the water starts to look cloudy or green. In a stable, buckets of water should be changed twice a day to keep the water fresh.

Extra goodness

Ponies need small amounts of some extra things too. A little salt and fat is necessary to keep their bodies healthy. Ready-mixed feeds such as pony nuts have the right amount of fat in them. Give your animals salt or mineral licks in their stalls or field. Ask your vet about vitamin supplements such as cod liver oil, especially in the winter.

Mineral licks can be popular with horses or ignored by them. Horses will use them only if they need them.

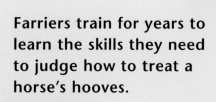

Farriers train for years to learn the skills they need to judge how to treat a horse's hooves.

Healthy feet

A big part of horse care is making sure the hooves are healthy. They work hard – such small feet carry such a great weight. Twice a day, and before and after every ride, you need to pick out your horse's hooves. A special hoof pick lets you dig stones, dirt, and mud out of the horse's feet.

A **farrier** will need to come and trim the hooves every four to eight weeks. Many horses and ponies have metal shoes nailed to their hooves to protect them on hard surfaces. The farrier will remove the shoe and trim the hoof. Then he or she will reshape the shoe or make a new one. Finally, the shoe is nailed back in place. The nails do not hurt, since the hoof at that point is like the dead fingernail growing past the end of your finger – the horse cannot feel it.

Checking your pony

You should check every day to see that your pony is healthy.

- Her ears should prick up when she sees you to show she is alert and curious.
- Her eyes should be bright, not weepy or crusty.
- Her nose should be dry.
- When she walks or runs, her legs should swing easily and her head should be held up.

If any of these things seem wrong, bring your pony in for a closer look.

Mucking out

Mucking out needs to be done every day. As well as picking up droppings in field shelters and **pastures**, you need to clean out the stable. Keeping **dung** out of the way will help keep your horse's feet healthy. It also controls **parasites** like **worms.** Worms and parasites live in dung. All horses have some worms and other parasites, but if they get out of control, your pony could lose weight and get sick.

The muck pile where you put droppings and used bedding should be somewhere close, but not too close to where people and animals spend a lot of time. Wash your hands well with soap after you have finished mucking out.

Step 1 – Get everything you need ready, and take your pony somewhere else secure.

Step 2 – Use a fork to lift up droppings and put them in the wheelbarrow.

Step 3 – Toss the dry bedding to the sides of the stable. Sweep up the wet bedding left on the floor and put it in the wheelbarrow. Leave the floor to dry.

Step 4 – Rake the bedding back over the floor. Leave it higher around the edges. Add as much fresh new bedding as you need.

Top tip

Horses are valuable and can be stolen. They can also go missing. Make sure yours can be identified easily by freeze marking or **microchipping** it. Both are painless. If you do microchip your horse, make sure you **register** it as well. Your vet should be able to give you advice.

Grooming and handling

Before you go for a ride, you need to get your horse or pony ready. Horses and ponies need to be **groomed** every time they are ridden, whether they live inside or outside. Grooming is what keeps the pony's skin and hair in good condition. It removes the dirt and dried sweat and keeps the skin clean enough to let fresh sweat run easily. It also helps keep the blood circulating well right under the skin. Grooming is also a great chance to check over every part of your horse, to make sure that he is healthy.

Ponies that live outside keep their skin healthy by rolling on the ground. They grow the right amount of hair for the seasons. The natural oils in their skins keep their hair healthy. It would disturb this balance for you to brush the coat too much, but you should remove mud or dried sweat.

Catching

The most difficult part of grooming a pony kept outside can be catching it! You should go to the field with a treat and the headcollar and lead rope. Get your pony's attention, then walk up to him showing the treat. As you reach your pony's left shoulder, put the lead rope around his neck. You can give him the treat as you put the headcollar on, still holding the lead rope firmly. When the headcollar is buckled on, lead the pony on his left side.

Always be confident when catching a pony in a field. Ask an expert for advice.

To lead a horse, hold the lead rope with one hand near the headcollar. Hold the end of the rope near your body in your other hand.

Learn the quick-release knot before you start working with horses.

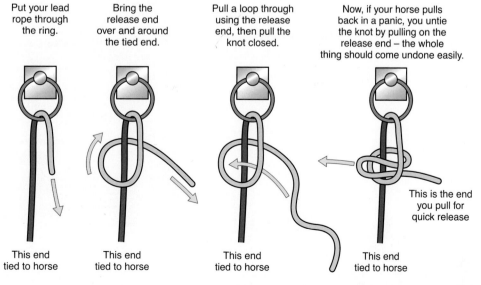

Put your lead rope through the ring.

Bring the release end over and around the tied end.

Pull a loop through using the release end, then pull the knot closed.

Now, if your horse pulls back in a panic, you untie the knot by pulling on the release end – the whole thing should come undone easily.

This is the end you pull for quick release

This end tied to horse

This end tied to horse

This end tied to horse

This end tied to horse

Before you ride

- If your pony lives in a stable, then catching him is easy. Tie him up securely, using a quick-release knot. Just give him a quick brush all over with the soft body brush to remove bedding. Pick out his hooves.
- A pony kept outside needs a stiff brush run over the places where the **tack** goes to make sure any dirt or mud is gone. Dirt would rub under the tack, and could irritate your pony's skin. He also needs his hooves picked out.
- Put the saddle cloth or **numnah** on. Gently place the saddle on and fasten the girth loosely. You will tighten it up properly right before you mount.
- Place the reins over your pony's neck. Remove the headcollar and lift the bridle up to his ears. Gently ask the horse to open his mouth for the bit. As you ease the headpiece over his ears, be careful. Some ponies hate having their ears touched. Fasten all the straps neatly so the ends do not flap as you ride.

bit

girth

numnah

Horses and ponies get bored and **stressed** on their own. A stable-mate is a good idea. Another horse or pony is ideal, but goats, cattle, and even cats can make good friends, too.

Top tips

- Horses and ponies like calm, steady behaviour. They are easily startled by flapping, shouting, and running.
- It is best to be slow and deliberate in everything you do.
- Show your horse new things before you use them, and let him smell them if you can.
- Make sure the pony can see you as you go near him – remember he cannot see behind his tail.
- To calm a startled pony, talk soothingly in a low voice. Stroke him firmly but gently along his neck or shoulder.

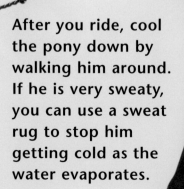

After you ride, cool the pony down by walking him around. If he is very sweaty, you can use a sweat rug to stop him getting cold as the water evaporates.

A full grooming routine

Ponies that live outside can be turned out in their fields after they have been ridden. They will roll in the field to cool themselves down. Ponies that live inside will need a full **grooming** when they have cooled down. They cannot keep their own skin healthy and rely on you to help them. They are often clipped in the winter, so their hair is shorter than it would be in the wild. They may need a rug to keep warm.

rubber curry comb

- Make sure your grooming kit is ready before you start. Remember to wash your kit every few weeks and never share between ponies.
- Start at the top on the left side of the neck. Do the whole left side, then the whole right side. Always use the same routine to groom.
- First use a rubber curry comb in a circular motion to loosen up any mud. Do not use the curry comb on the legs, or places where the bones are near the skin.
- Then use the stiff dandy brush to lift the dirt. You can clean mud off the legs with this brush. Follow with the softer body brush all over. Brush the head with the body brush, too.
- Use the body brush to ease tangles out of the mane and tail.
- Use one sponge to wash the dock area under the horse's tail. Use another sponge to wipe the nose, eyes, and lips. It helps if these sponges are different colours!

- Pick the hooves out. Be careful not to hurt the **frog**. You can then paint them with hoof oil if you like, but not every day since hooves also need some air.
- Finally rub all over with the stable rubber to take any last dirt off and give the coat a shine.
- Wash your hands when you have finished.

hoof pick

If it is very warm and your pony gets very sweaty during your ride, you can give him a bath afterwards. You can also just sponge or hose off the saddle area instead. Always keep your horse warm while he dries.

Top tips

When should you not lead a horse to water?

- When a horse has been working hard, offer him half a bucket of water. Do not give him more until he has cooled down.
- Make sure you offer your horse water before giving him **hard feeds**.
- Never let a horse drink from a pond, lake, or stream if the water looks green, cloudy, sandy, still, or if it smells bad.

37

Seeing the vet

Before you even get a horse or pony, find a good horse vet. Ask friends and people at riding stables who they recommend. A good vet will understand that you want to learn more about your horse. You may want to make a list of things to discuss with the vet during routine check ups. Make sure you have a good idea of the charges for routine care and emergency call outs too. If there is an emergency, an adult will need to call the vet.

Vaccinations for a horse are like the ones given to people, but the syringes can look much bigger!

An adult should be there whenever the vet is treating your horse or if you need to do any treatments yourself.

About once a year, your horse or pony will need a check up with your vet. You can expect the vet to:

- check the pony's temperature, pulse, and breathing to make sure they are normal
- watch the pony trot, to make sure that she is not **lame**
- feel the pony's legs and around other parts of the body to check for heat or swelling
- look at the teeth and rasp, or 'float', them to grind sharp bits down and even them up
- give **vaccinations** – usually tetanus and equine flu, but others may also be a good idea depending on where you live.

The vet uses a gag to hold a horse's mouth open. The rasp looks painful but doesn't hurt your horse at all.

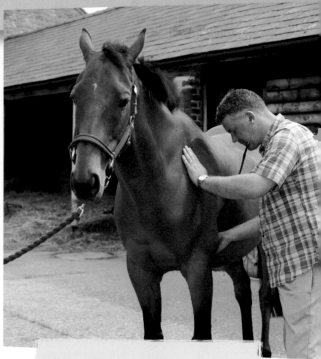

The vet will check your horse all over to make sure she is healthy.

Worms

The vet may also want to test a sample of **dung** for **intestinal worms.** You can then use the correct treatment for the worms and kill them off effectively. You will need to use a paste or powder wormer every eight to thirteen weeks. Your vet can help you plan your worming for the following months.

When should you call the vet?

If your horse or pony is injured or seems very ill, call the vet immediately. But if she just seems not quite herself, it can be harder to decide. Generally, until you know your horse very well and have a great deal of experience with horses, it is a good idea to ask an adult to call the vet if you are worried. Note down any worrying symptoms and ask the vet what other information might help.

Some health problems

It is a good idea to know the types of health problem horses and ponies can have. Most problems happen with the legs and feet.

- **Lameness** – This can be caused by many things, such as stones in the feet, a bang on the leg or a bone problem. There may be heat or swelling, or the leg may look normal. A lame horse will not want to put weight on the lame foot or leg. She will trot unevenly. Ask an expert how to treat the kind of lameness you see, since treatment depends on the cause.

- Bot-fly eggs – The female bot fly lays her eggs on a horse's legs in the summer. They look like small yellow spots. You need to get them off with a special scraper or knife. Ask an adult for help with this. Left alone, the pony may lick the eggs and get the **larvae** in her body when they hatch.

- Thrush – This often happens if a pony stands in dirty bedding. The **frog** (springy part) of the foot gets swollen and starts to smell very bad. It is treated by keeping the horse in clean, dry bedding and using a special medicine. Sometimes the **farrier** can cut out the bad bits of the frog.

First aid

People who look after horses need to learn to clean and dress a wound, bandage a leg, hose an injured leg or foot, and put a **poultice** on a foot. The only way to learn these skills is from an expert, and with practice. Make sure an adult at your stable knows how to do them. Ask your vet what medicines you should have in your first aid kit. You will also need bandages, tape, cotton wool, scissors, and a thermometer.

- Mud fever – This happens when a pony stands on wet ground for too long. The skin on the heels gets chapped, then it cracks. The hair falls out and the wounds get infected. The vet will need to give you a special cream to treat the scabs. Moving the pony to dry land is the only way to keep it from happening again.
- Laminitis – This is also called founder. It can happen when a pony eats too much lush spring grass or new fresh hay. Usually just the front feet get very hot right inside the hoof. It hurts a lot. If you think your pony has laminitis, call the vet at once. You can stand her in cold water to help cool the feet and make it hurt less.

It takes time to learn how to do a leg bandage this well.

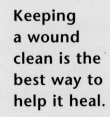

Keeping a wound clean is the best way to help it heal.

41

Colic

Horses and ponies have delicate digestive systems. If they eat too much, or if you change their diets suddenly, they can get colic. The pony may bite at its side, look uneasy, paw or roll, and swish his tail. Colic is basically a stomach ache, and can usually be fixed with medicine from the vet. But it is important to call the vet at once – untreated colic can kill a horse.

Coughs and wheezes

A horse may get a cough for a number of reasons. When a cough happens, stop working your pony. Ask the vet what to do. If you exercise a pony with a cough, you could damage its lungs forever. Doing so could cause a permanent wheeze called "broken wind".

Paste wormer is pushed through a syringe into the back of the horse's mouth.

Sweet itch

Almost all ponies rub their manes and tails against posts, trees, and anything solid they can find from time to time. But if a pony is rubbing a lot, it may have sweet itch. This is caused by midge bites. You can treat it with special cream from the vet, and also keep the horse in at dusk and dawn, when the midges bite the most.

Building knowledge

If any of your friends' ponies get a common disease, ask to see what the symptoms look like and how it is treated. Then you will be adding to your knowledge.

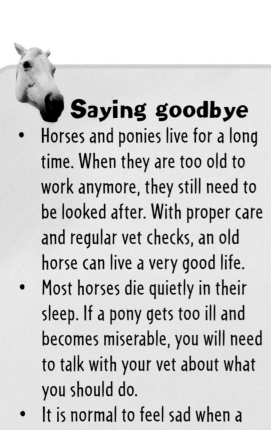

Saying goodbye

- Horses and ponies live for a long time. When they are too old to work anymore, they still need to be looked after. With proper care and regular vet checks, an old horse can live a very good life.

- Most horses die quietly in their sleep. If a pony gets too ill and becomes miserable, you will need to talk with your vet about what you should do.

- It is normal to feel sad when a pet dies. After time passes, the pain will lessen. Then you will be able to remember the fun times you had with your pony.

Sweet itch not only makes the horse miserable, but it looks bad too.

An old horse can be a wonderful stable-mate for a younger horse.

Keeping a record

Even before you decide to get your own horse or pony, you can start keeping a scrapbook. There is so much to learn about horses. You could divide your book into sections about horse care, stable management, breeds and **conformation**, riding, and anything else you want. As you learn more, you can add notes and pictures.

Keep your scrapbook up to date with news about your horse's health, funny things she does, and shows you have been to. Make sure you caption your photos so you can remember the important things about them.

Record change

When you do get your own pony, take a lot of notes. You can write down what she eats, how big she is, what equipment you have for her, and what her daily routine is. Try to record the funny things she does as well!

As you grow together, your routine will change. Notes mean you can look back at the changes and think about new ways to do things. It is also very wise to keep detailed health notes. Write about routine check ups, worming, and **vaccinations**, as well as emergencies and how you dealt with them.

A scrapbook is a great place to put photos and rosettes so you can remember everyday and special events. You can show friends your scrapbook even if they cannot meet your pony in person.

Keep learning

Even when you are a good rider, and your horse is well trained, you should both keep learning to stay interested. You can use shows as goals to work towards. Special training workshops and regular riding lessons will keep your skills improving, too.

When you go to shows and riding events called gymkhanas, you may win rosettes or even trophies. They are fun to display. They help you remember the good times you had and the goals you met.

Glossary

allergic   when someone reacts badly to something they eat, breathe or get stung by

ancestors   animal's parents, grandparents, and all the other animals it is descended from

bridlepaths   special routes through the countryside and along roads meant to be used by horses and riders

conformation   how the horse is built

dung   droppings from a horse or pony

farrier   person who looks after horses' feet

favour   to keep weight off part of the body that is hurting

foals   baby horses

frog   soft, springy, v-shaped part of a horse's foot that cushions it from the shock as it hits the ground

gelding   neutered male horse

grain   food for horses

graze   eat grass or hay almost constantly

groom   to clean and polish

hands   way to measure height in horses – a hand is 10 centimetres (4 inches)

hard feeds   grain-based food

hemp   herb that has a lot of fibre in it

herbivores   plant eaters

herd   group of horses

insurance   when you agree to pay a company a regular amount of money and they agree to pay certain bills if you have an accident or emergency

intestinal worms   tiny parasites that live inside the digestive system of an animal

intestines   digestive system of horses

lame   when a horse's leg or foot is injured and will not take the animal's weight, making it move awkwardly

larvae   wormlike young of many insects

livery stable   stable that takes boarding ponies, often feeding and caring for them

loose-box   stall large enough for a horse to lie down in comfortably

mammals   animals that give birth to babies and feed them on milk

microchipping   when a very small computer chip that holds a lot of information is put under the animal's skin

mucking out   cleaning out a horse's stall

neutered   having an operation that stops an animal from having babies

numnah   special blanket put under a horse's saddle

nutrients   the things in food that animals and plants need to keep healthy

paddock   smaller fenced-in field a horse or pony grazes in

parasites   small creatures, such as worms or mites, that live on or in another creature

pasture   field for grazing

pecking order   way a herd is ranked

pedigree   horse that is pure-bred and has records of its family tree

poultice   soft mixture of soothing ingredients such as bran or clay that is mixed with hot water and bandaged onto a bruise or abscess to help it heal

registered   when an animal's details are recorded by a national or international organization

reining   Western riding style where the horse is directed by the rider's shifting body weight and the feel of the reins on the side of its neck

shelter   place where abandoned animals are cared for until they find a new home

stressed   made tense by feeling bad or worried in body or mind

tack   equipment a horse wears when being ridden, such as saddle and bridle

trotted out   when a horse is allowed to trot along with someone running alongside

vaccinations   injections that help protect against diseases

warm-blooded   animal that is able to create its own body heat

worms   parasites that live in other animals

Further reading

Horse Care for Kids, Cherry Hill (Storey Books, 2002)

Kingfisher Riding Club: Horse and Pony Care, Sandy Ransford (Kingfisher, 2002)

Pony Care (A Young Rider's Guide), Carolyn Henderson (Dorling Kindersley, 2005)

The Manual of Horsemanship 13th Edition, Barbara Cooper (The Pony Club, 2005)

Useful addresses

Most countries have organizations and societies that work to protect animals from cruelty and to help people learn how to care for the pets they live with properly.

UK
Royal Society for the Prevention of
    Cruelty to Animals (RSPCA)
Wilberforce Way
Southwater
Horsham
West Sussex
RH13 9RS
Tel: 0870 33 35 999
Fax: 0870 75 30 284

Australia
RSPCA Australia Inc
PO Box 265
Deakin West ACT 2600
Australia
Tel: 02 6282 8300
Fax: 02 6282 8311

Internet
The Pony Club
http://www.pcuk.org/

The British Horse Society
www.bhs.org.uk

Western-style riding
www.wes-uk.com and
www.horsearound.co.uk

RSPCA
www.rspca.org.uk

This is an international specialist horse site:
www.equiworld.net

Australia
RSPCA
www.rspca.org.au

Equestrian Federation of Australia
www.efanational.com

Disclaimer
All the Internet addresses (URLs) given in this book were valid at the time of going to press. However, due to the dynamic nature of the Internet, some addresses may have changed, or sites may have changed or ceased to exist since publication. While the author and Publishers regret any inconvenience this may cause readers, no responsibility for any such changes can be accepted by either the author or the Publishers.

Index